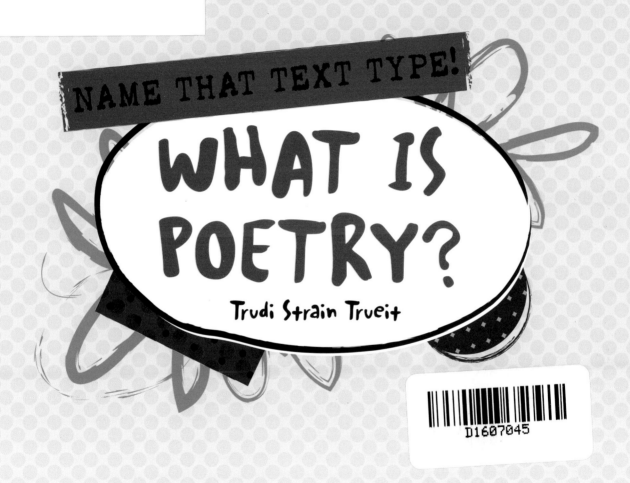

NAME THAT TEXT TYPE!

WHAT IS POETRY?

Trudi Strain Trueit

Lerner Publications Company • Minneapolis

To my mom, Shirley, who always hung my poetry on the refrigerator door. Everyone needs a champion. I had the best.

Lerner Publications Company
A division of Lerner Publishing Group, Inc.
241 First Avenue North
Minneapolis, MN 55401 USA

For reading levels and more information, look up this title at www.lernerbooks.com.

The poems "Fall King," "First Snowfall," "Get Me off This Thing!," "The Girl with the Tasty Hair," "LIFE," "Stardust," and all untitled poems not otherwise credited © by Lerner Publishing Group, Inc. All rights reserved.

Main body text set in Avenir LT Pro 15/21. Typeface provided by Linotype AG.

Library of Congress Cataloging-in-Publication Data

Trueit, Trudi Strain.
    What is poetry? / Trudi Strain Trueit.
        p.   cm. — (Name that text type!)
    Includes index.
    ISBN 978–1–4677–3667–1 (lib. bdg. : alk. paper)
    ISBN 978–1–4677–4703–5 (eBook)
    1. Poetry—Juvenile literature. I. Title.
PN1031.T73 2015
808.1—dc23   2013039056

Manufactured in the United States of America
1 – BP – 7/15/14

Contents

Many people get poetry for their birthdays. Do you? Does your family sing "Happy Birthday"? The lyrics are poetry. Do you get birthday cards? Sometimes the notes in the cards are poetry.

**You are one year older
and one year nicer too.
But I'm the lucky one
to have a friend like you!**

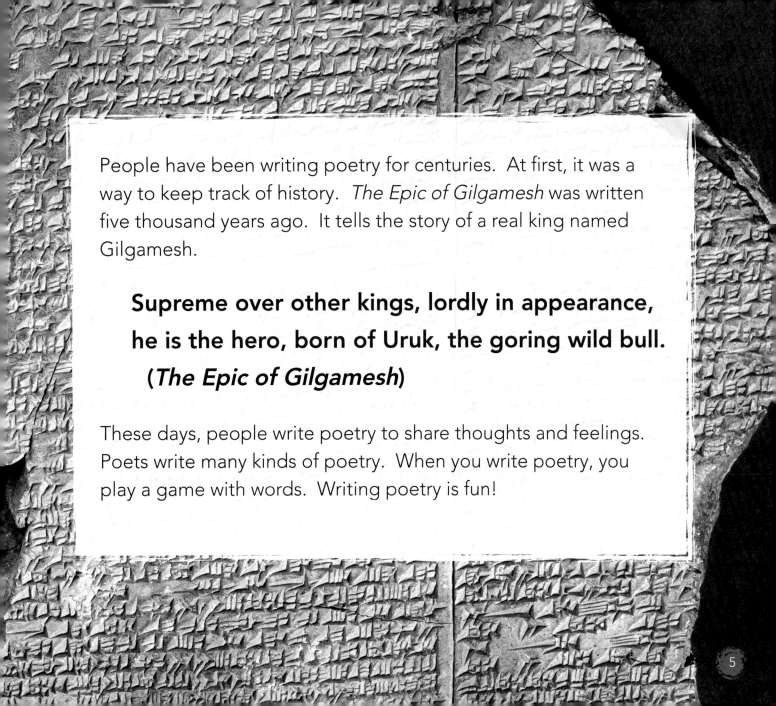

People have been writing poetry for centuries. At first, it was a way to keep track of history. *The Epic of Gilgamesh* was written five thousand years ago. It tells the story of a real king named Gilgamesh.

Supreme over other kings, lordly in appearance,

he is the hero, born of Uruk, the goring wild bull.

(*The Epic of Gilgamesh*)

These days, people write poetry to share thoughts and feelings. Poets write many kinds of poetry. When you write poetry, you play a game with words. Writing poetry is fun!

EXPLORING POETRY

Poetry isn't like other kinds of writing. Why? First, most poems don't have long sentences. A poem has lines. A line may be a word or two. It may be the first part of an idea. The next line finishes the idea.

Some poems have a set number of lines. A group of lines is called a stanza. A quatrain has four lines in each stanza. The poem "First Snowfall" is a quatrain.

First Snowfall

"Pardon me, Teacher?"
No talking, I know.
"Just look! Outside!
It's starting to snow!"

Hurry up, recess.
I've got a plan.
I'll use every flake
to build a snowman.

Poetry may also have a rhythm. That's a pattern of beats. Each syllable is a beat. All the lines in a poem may have the same number of syllables. Or line 1 will have the same number of syllables as line 3. Line 2 will have the same number of syllables as line 4.

Some syllables in poetry are stressed. Read the next stanza of "First Snowfall" aloud. Say the underlined syllables louder than the rest. Clap as you say these stressed words. This will help you pick up the rhythm.

I **<u>beg</u>** and I **<u>plead</u>**.
But **<u>teach</u>**er says, "**<u>Wait</u>!**"
And **<u>when</u>** the bell **<u>rings</u>**,
I **<u>rush</u>** to my **<u>fate</u>**.

How words sound is important in poetry. A poet picks words that sound good together. A poet may pick words that rhyme. *Rhyming* means "to use words that sound alike." Some rhyming words have the same letters, like "know" and "snow." Other rhyming words have different letters that sound the same, such as "awful" and "waffle." Read the rest of "First Snowfall" aloud. Listen to the sounds. Which words rhyme?

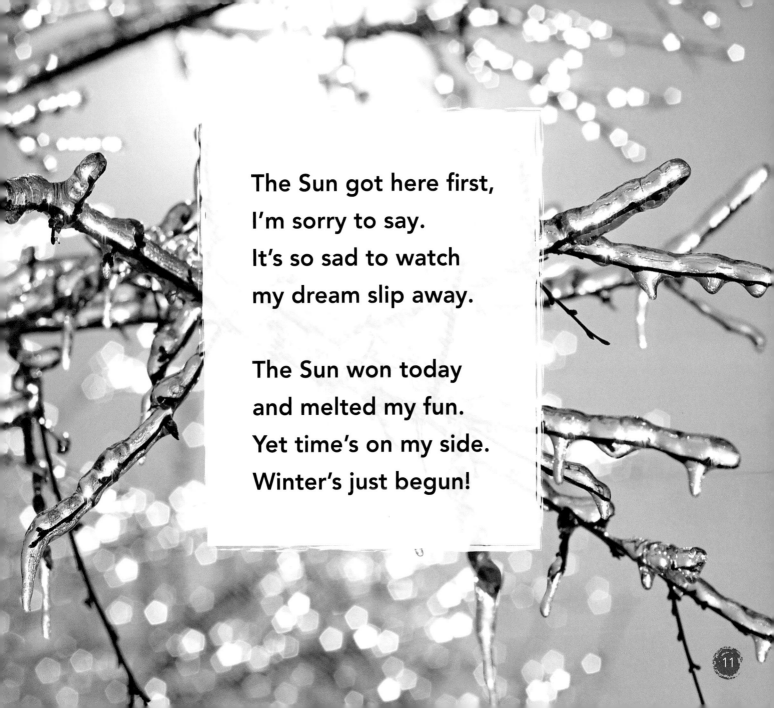

The Sun got here first,
I'm sorry to say.
It's so sad to watch
my dream slip away.

The Sun won today
and melted my fun.
Yet time's on my side.
Winter's just begun!

Poetry doesn't have to follow rules. Free verse poetry has no rules. It may have any number of lines or stanzas. Free verse has no special rhythm. It may or may not rhyme. The poet gets to decide these things. "Get Me off This Thing!" is a free verse poem.

Get Me off This Thing!

Inching up the hill toward our doom.

Up, up, up!

Bad idea.

Bad, bad, bad idea.

Shut eyes. Hold on. Don't hurl.

Teetering at the peak.

No sound, no air, no breath.

Nothing.

Eyes open. Wide. It's so far . . .

Down, down, down!

Swerve left.

Skin glued to bones.

Swerve right.

Hair spun like cotton candy.

Loop-de-loop-de-loop-de-loop.

Did my eyeballs fall out?

Slowing, slowing,

slooooooooooowing

Stop.

Can we go again?

IDEAS AT PLAY

Poetry often has a subject. Many poets write about feelings. Some poets write about life. They use their senses. They look, listen, smell, taste, and touch.

Through the ample open door of the peaceful country barn,
A sunlit pasture field with cattle and horses feeding,
And haze and vista, and the far horizon fading away.
(Walt Whitman, "A Farm Picture")

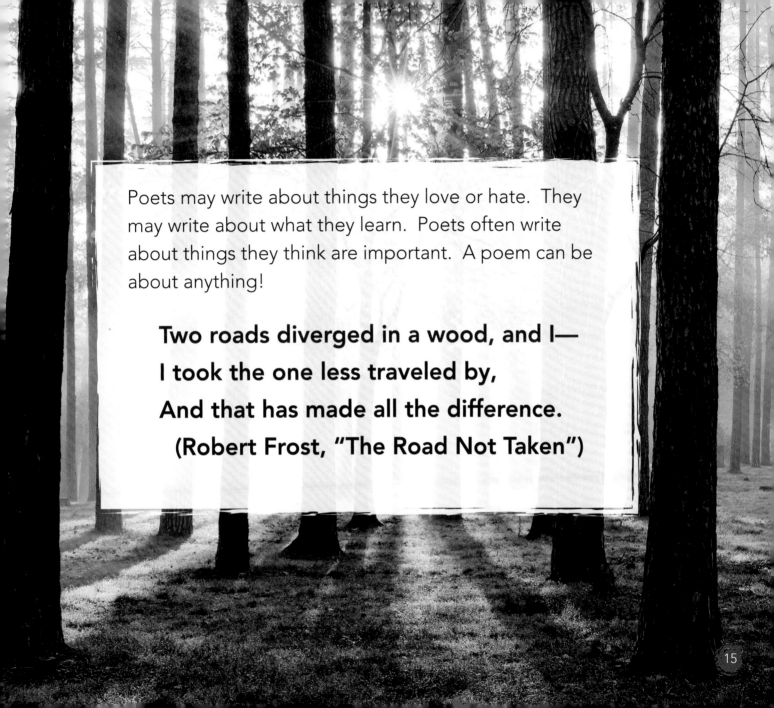

Poets may write about things they love or hate. They may write about what they learn. Poets often write about things they think are important. A poem can be about anything!

Two roads diverged in a wood, and I—
I took the one less traveled by,
And that has made all the difference.
(Robert Frost, "The Road Not Taken")

Sometimes poets use writing tools to help them craft a poem. One tool is alliteration. It means to put together words that start with the same letter or sound. What letter is used in this example?

Sunflower sways to September's song.

"Summer will soon be gone," sings September.

Sunflower sighs.

Poets may also use simile and metaphor. A simile compares two things. It uses the connecting words "like" or "as if."

The giraffe is *like* a tower, strong and true.

Metaphor doesn't use connecting words. Instead, it says one thing *is* the other. Here's an example:

The giraffe *is* a tower, strong and true.

Onomatopoeia means "to use a word that sounds like what the word means." *Woof* and *bang* are examples.

Poets may also repeat a word, a phrase, or a stanza. Repetition may help the rhythm or the sound. Try to find onomatopoeia and repetition in "Fall King."

Fall King

Scrunch! Scrunch!
Autumn's grand carpet
Rolled out for you and me.
A patchwork of gold and red and orange
Rolled out to the corners of the Earth.
Scrunch! Scrunch!
Do you hear? They're asking us to pile them,
Pile them,
Pile them high!
I am free, I am happy, I am king.
Let's jump in!

Poets may draw pictures with words. A concrete poem mixes poetry and art. The words in a concrete poem take the shape of the subject. A poet writing about love might put the words in the shape of a heart.

LIFE

Waste one day then *another*
and another and *another*
and before you
know it you
are out
of
t
i
3

e

learn guitar play dance
read soccer journal
take a great book volunteer

A PARADE OF POEMS

There are many types of poetry. Some kinds have rules. Let's look at some kinds of poems and their rules.

A nursery rhyme is often the first poem we learn. It's a short poem or song. It tells a simple story. It usually rhymes. "Jack and Jill" is a nursery rhyme.

Jack and Jill

Jack and Jill went up the hill
To fetch a pail of water;
Jack fell down and broke his crown,
And Jill came tumbling after.

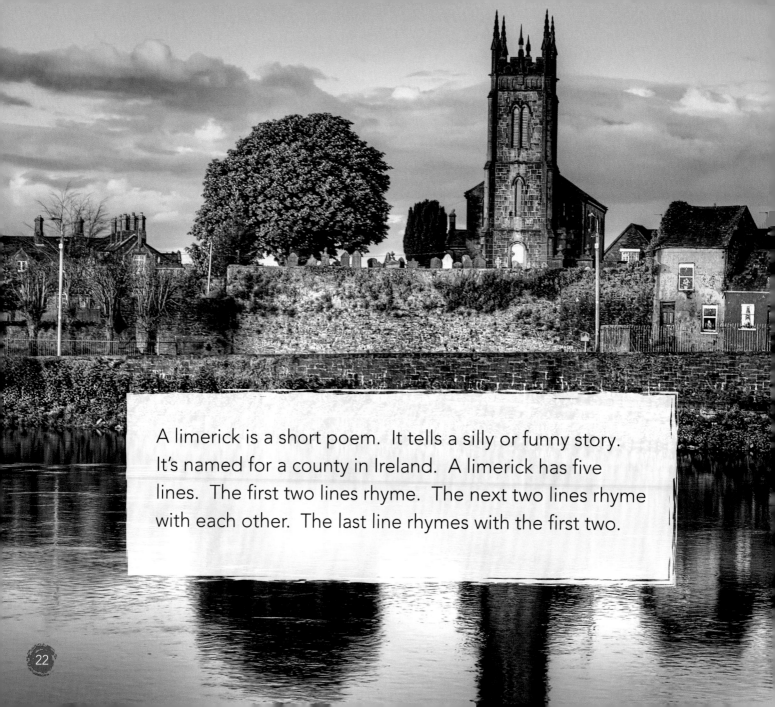

A limerick is a short poem. It tells a silly or funny story. It's named for a county in Ireland. A limerick has five lines. The first two lines rhyme. The next two lines rhyme with each other. The last line rhymes with the first two.

The Girl with the Tasty Hair

I once knew a girl named Claire.

She had noodles for hair.

She added some sauce,

and with a quick toss,

Our dinner was all prepared!

A narrative poem tells a story. It may be a true story or a legend. Narrative poems often rhyme. But they don't have to. This kind of poem may be any length. Some are as long as books! "Stardust" is a narrative poem.

Stardust

No one heard her stomach growl.
She had no tag. No name.
She pawed through trash for scraps to eat.
She slept out in the rain.
Until one day a hand reached out,
a bit of food to give.
Could she trust this one enough
to change the way she lived?
No struggle lasts forever,
say eyes, now free of pain.
She is mine and I am hers.
Stardust is her name.

Haiku is a type of poetry from Japan. It has three lines. The first and third lines have five syllables each. The second line has seven syllables. Haiku doesn't usually rhyme. Its subject is almost always nature. This kind of poem is not titled.

Sun, that old charmer
Bends to kiss bashful blossom
The world awakens

An acrostic poem is like a crossword puzzle. The first letter of each line forms a word when read downward. The word is the subject of the poem.

Person, young or

Old, unafraid to

Express what is hidden, unafraid to

Tell the world a truth

16   17   18
20   21   22   23
6   29
38   40
3   48
59   62
65   66   67   68
69   70   71   72   73
78   79   80   81   82   83

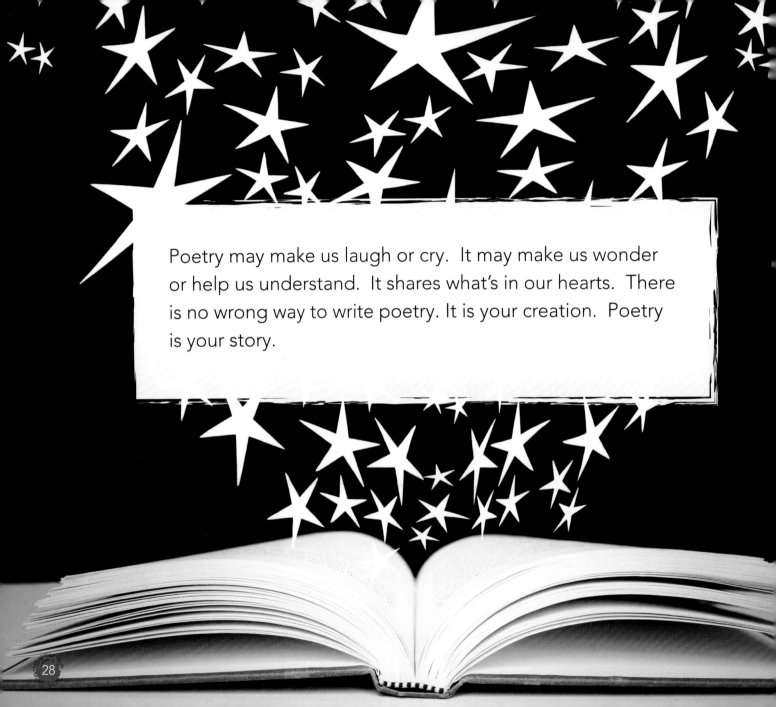

Poetry may make us laugh or cry. It may make us wonder or help us understand. It shares what's in our hearts. There is no wrong way to write poetry. It is your creation. Poetry is your story.

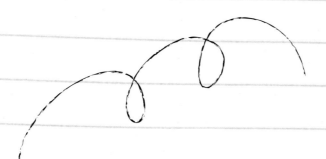

Now You Do It

Craft your own acrostic poem. Choose a friend to write about. Make a list of words or phrases about your friend. Next, write the friend's name down the left edge of a page. Put one letter on each line. Use your list to write lines that start with those letters. Remember, the lines do not need to rhyme.

Read your poem out loud. Are you happy with the sound? Change words you don't like. If you get stuck, put the poem away. Come back to it later. You will likely have new ideas when you do.

Glossary

alliteration: a group of words that start with the same letter or sound

lyrics: the words of a song

metaphor: a word or phrase that compares two things. A metaphor does not use "like" or "as if."

onomatopoeia: a word that sounds like what it means, like *pop* or *meow*

quatrain: a poem with four lines in each stanza

rhyme: when words sound alike. *Blue* and *clue* rhyme.

rhythm: the pattern of beats made by a poem's syllables

simile: a word or phrase that compares two things using the words "like" or "as if"

stanza: a group of lines in a poem

syllable: a part of a word. The word *syllable* has three syllables.

Further Information

Cleary, Brian P. *If It Rains Pancakes: Haiku and Lantern Poems.* Minneapolis: Millbrook Press, 2014. Haiku and lanterns are two types of ancient Japanese poetry. The poems in this book will make you chuckle, puzzle, and ponder . . . and inspire you to write your own!

Kenn Nesbitt's Poetry 4 Kids
http://www.poetry4kids.com
This website from children's poet laureate Kenn Nesbitt is bursting with ideas for writing all kinds of poetry. Use the online rhyming dictionary to find rhymes for your own verses.

Poets House Children's Room
http://www.poetshouse.org/childrens-room
Click on the "inspiration station" to help you jump-start your own writing. Save your poems on this site, and read poetry written by other kids.

Prelutsky, Jack. *Read a Rhyme, Write a Rhyme.* New York: Dragonfly Books, 2009. Learn how to write poetry by finishing some of the poems in this interactive poetry book! It includes poetry-writing tips and lists of rhyming words.

Salas, Laura Purdie. *Water Can Be . . .* Minneapolis: Millbrook Press, 2014. Discover how a poet uses a familiar subject and rhyme to tell an interesting and beautiful story.

LERNER
SOURCE
Expand learning beyond the printed book. Download free, complementary educational resources for this book from our website, www.lernerresource.com.

Index

Photo Acknowledgments

The images in this book are used with the permission of: © Shutterstock.com, p. 2, 30, 31, 32; © Ruth Black/Shutterstock.com, p. 4; © Leemage/Getty Images, p. 5; © Smit/Shutterstock.com, p. 6; © Triff/Shutterstock.com, p. 7; © Szasz-Fabian Ilka Erika/Shutterstock.com, p. 8; © Phillip Dyhr Hobbs/Shutterstock.com, p. 9; © Lydmyla Kharlamova/Shutterstock.com, p. 10; © Plus69/Shutterstock.com, p. 11; © Marcio Jose Bastos Silva/Shutterstock.com, p. 12; © iStockphoto.com/Karen Mower, p. 13; © Scott Prokop/Shutterstock.com, p. 14; © Mny-Jhee/Shutterstock.com, p. 15; © gornjak/Shutterstock.com, p. 16; © Eric Gevaert/Shutterstock.com, p. 17; © Miao Liao/Shutterstock.com, p. 18; © iStockphoto.com/eyewave, p. 20; © Ryan Simpson/Shutterstock.com, p. 21; © Patryk Kosmider/Shutterstock.com, p. 22; © Viktor1/Shutterstock.com, p. 23; © Hemera/Thinkstock, p. 24; © Leszek Glasner/Shutterstock.com, p. 25; © AVprophoto/Shutterstock.com, p. 26; © Losswen/Shutterstock.com, p. 27; © Valentina Photos/Shutterstock.com, p. 28; © Photoraidz/Shutterstock.com, p. 29.

Cover: © mcherevan/Shutterstock.com, (black writing) ; © robert_s/Shutterstock.com (ipad); © Seregam/Shutterstock.com (notebook); © Vitaly Korovin/Shutterstock.com (pencil); © Nina_Susik/Shutterstock.com (gray writing).